THE LANGUID GOAT IS ALWAYS THIN

D0313570

First published in 2001 by Prion Books Ltd
Imperial Works, Perren Street
London NW5 3ED
www.prionbooks.com

Reprinted 2001 and 2002

ISBN 1-85375-432-3

Cover design by Jon Gray
Printed & bound in China by
Everbest Printing

THE LANGUID GOAT IS ALWAYS THIN

the world's strangest proverbs

Compiled by
STEPHEN ARNOTT

PRION

Empty gossip
jumps with one leg

ESTONIAN

Dry pants catch no fish

BULGARIAN

You cannot prevent the birds of
sadness from flying over your head,
but you can prevent them
from nesting in your hair

CHINESE

With patience and saliva
the ant swallows the elephant

COLOMBIAN

After being struck on the head
by an axe, it is a positive pleasure
to be beaten about the body
with a wooden club

CHINESE

Mistakes ain't haystacks
or there'd be more fat ponies
than there is

UNITED STATES

Alms once given is as phlegm
which has been expectorated:
not worth taking back

KUMAUNI (INDIA)

The tongue is soft and constantly
remains in; the teeth are hard
and fall out

CHINESE

Nothing to bother you, eh?
Then go and buy a goat

INDIAN

Scabby donkeys scent each other
over nine hills

BULGARIAN

He who fondles you more than
usual has either deceived you
or wishes to do so

FRENCH

If two men keep a horse, it is thin;
if two families keep a boat, it leaks

CHINESE

If you throw cakes at a man
he will throw cakes at you

JAPANESE

One who is tempted today
by a cucumber will be tempted
tomorrow by a goat

KUMAUNI (INDIA)

The smaller the lizard,
the greater its hopes of
becoming a crocodile

ETHIOPIAN

When you see a village with nine
houses and ten inns, flee from it

BULGARIAN

First he asks for your
walking stick, then he wants
your pet daughter

KASHMIRI (INDIA)

Thy friend has a friend,
and thy friend's friend has
a friend — be discreet

HEBREW

Kiss the hand you cannot bite

ROMANIAN

The ground is always
frozen for lazy pigs

DANISH

He who depends on people
hangs from a tree

GERMAN

Although there exist many thousands of subjects for elegant conversation, there are persons who cannot meet a cripple without talking about feet

CHINESE

The leper is prepared to swear
on behalf of his fellow inmates
that, should he go on a journey, none
of them would ever dream of borrowin
his bath sponge during his absence

YORUBA

Lying a little, stealing a little, will
get you nicely through the world

ESTONIAN

Whoever has never seen a tiger
let him look at a cat, and whoever
has never seen a robber
let him look at a butcher

URDU

Being a baker is poor work
if your head is made of butter

DANISH

Badly cut hair is two men's shame

DANISH

Thrash your apprentice while he
has not yet broken the water jug

BULGARIAN

Barbers, doctors, pleaders,
prostitutes: all must
have cash down

INDIAN

A piece of paper blown by the
wind into the law-court may
in the end only be drawn out
again by two oxen

CHINESE

The doctor cures the sick man
who does not die

JAPANESE

The inexperienced physician
makes a lumpy churchyard

CZECH

Beware of men without beards
and women with beards

BASQUE

When one is past thirty
one can about half
comprehend the weather

CHINESE

When youth takes the scorpion
for a bed-fellow, the aged
go out on the roof

CHINESE

Ask the opinion of an older one
and a younger one than thyself,
and return to thine opinion

EGYPTIAN

There are only two things
a girl chooses for herself —
her potatoes and her lover

DUTCH

A woman's advice is never worth having, yet no one but a fool refuses to follow it

SPANISH

She who wields a
big wooden ladle
rules all

BHOJPURI

With a woman's tongue
and a curé's hat one
makes a wonderful
pair of shoes

BULGARIAN

If a woman were as small as
she is good, one could make her
a whole dress and crown
out of a leaf of parsley

FRENCH

A guest is a fowl —
he will soon have his neck wrung

BONDEI (EAST AFRICA)

People of seventy you should not keep overnight, and do not invite a person of eighty to sit down

CHINESE

You may laugh at a friend's
roof; don't laugh at his
sleeping accommodation

BONDEI (EAST AFRICA)

The fish and the guest
go bad on the third day
and must be thrown out

BASQUE

When your wife tells you to
jump off a roof, pray God
that it is a low one

SPANISH

A good-looking wife
is the world's,
an ugly one your own

MARATHI

If the husband gathers with
a fan and the woman scatters
with a spoon, there will
never be a heap

ALBANIAN

He who knocks his wife about
thoroughly will be forgiven
a hundred sins

ESTONIAN

Consult thy wife and do
the reverse of what she says

TUNISIAN

It is easier to bear a child
once a year than
to shave every day

RUSSIAN

A wife is twice kind —
on her wedding day
and at her funeral

RUSSIAN

Hairy husband – smooth happiness

ESTONIAN

Do not blow in a bear's ear

BASQUE

Do not praise a day before sunset,
a horse before a year,
and a wife before she's dead

CZECH

A wife will be doubly attached
if her chain is pleasant

EYGPTIAN

Trust your bitch sooner
than your pretty wife

BULGARIAN

Many children, wide ears

ESTONIAN

Spank small buttocks
that large buttocks
may not be flogged

BULGARIAN

The daughters of the house
are nothing but ornaments
of the front garden
and articles for sale

ESTONIAN

If you love your son,
give him plenty of cudgel:
if you hate him,
cram him with dainties

BULGARIAN

Comb your daughter's hair
until she is twelve, safeguard
her until she is sixteen,
after sixteen say 'thank you'
to whomsoever will wed her

CZECH

A mother-in-law, like the
Yucca tree, is useful underground

CUBAN

I speak to you,
O daughter-in-law,
that you may hear,
O neighbour

EGYPTIAN

You cannot buy honourable
rice from a dead uncle

CHINESE

'Two brothers against a bear,
and two brothers-in-law
at a milk pudding

RUSSIAN

Nobody's family can hang up the sign 'Nothing the Matter ~Here'

CHINESE

Confide in an aunt
and the world will know

CZECH

If we are brothers
our purses are not sisters

BULGARIAN

In the time of need
the pig is called uncle

ALBANIAN

He on whose head we
would break a coconut
never stands still

YORUBA (WEST AFRICA)

Two lords are going to have
a fight: farmers lend your hair

CZECH

When you shake hands with
a Greek, count your fingers

ALBANIAN

If a man of Naresh has
kissed thee, count thy teeth

HEBREW

A hungry Frenchman
welcomes a crow

RUSSIAN

Trust a snake before a Jew,
a Jew before a Greek,
but never an Armenian

FRENCH

If you hate a man, let him live

Hang a German
even if he is a good man

RUSSIAN

Do not trust a Hungarian unless
he has a third eye in his forehead

CZECH

Good luck is an
eel in the pond of fools

RUSSIAN

Throw the fortunate man
into the Nile and he will come
out with a fish in his mouth

EYGPTIAN

Who has got luck need only
sit at home with his mouth open

GERMAN

Give me, mother, luck at birth
then throw me if you will
on the rubbish heap

BULGARIAN

A rich man's sickness and
a poor man's pancake
are smelt a long way off

FLEMISH

There is no economy in going
to bed early to save candles
if the result be twins

CHINESE

He who has gold is beloved,
though he be a dog
and a son of a dog

TUNISIAN

Lending to a spendthrift
is like pelting a trespassing dog
with meat dumplings

CHINESE

If a low-bred man
obtains wealth, he will carry
an umbrella at midnight

TAMIL (INDIA)

Accept even chaff and
a sterile goat from
him who pays badly

CZECH

Mr Immortal is dead,
Mr Possessor-of-Wealth is
begging, Mrs Riches is
gathering cow-dung cakes, so
Mr Owner-of-Nothing is best of all

MARATHI (INDIA)

Brotherly love for brotherly love,
but cheese for money

ALBANIAN

Father a grocer,
son a gentleman,
grandson a beggar

PERUVIAN

Love, a cough, smoke and money
cannot long be hid

FRENCH

With money you can even
buy rabbit-cheese

ROMANIAN

If misfortune has not found you,
wait a minute, you'll find it

BULGARIAN

If you wish to be blamed, marry;
if you wish to be praised, die

GALLA (NORTH AFRICA)

He who thinks he is raising
a mound may only in reality
be digging a pit

CHINESE

He who washes a beautiful
goat seldom milks it

CHUANA (SOUTH AFRICA)

Almonds come to those
who have no teeth

CHINESE

When God wills the destruction
of an ant, he gives it wings

IRAQI

He that builds bridges and repairs roads will become blind in both eyes; he that commits murder and arson will enjoy long life

CHINESE

He who is not yet dead
is not yet clear of defects

KENYAN

He who has nobody to tie him up
should not go mad

YORUBA

Drink and sing: an inch before
us is black night

JAPANESE

The man who tickles himself
can laugh when he chooses

GERMAN

When your head does not work
your legs suffer

ROMANIAN

A slice of ham is better
than a fat pig in a dream

GERMAN

Two men are frightened of
an unloaded gun

BULGARIAN

He who can read and write
has four eyes

ALBANIAN

One hears pedestrians
sing most of the riding songs

RUSSIAN

To tell the truth is dangerous;
to listen to it is annoying

DANISH

Creaking wagons
are long in passing

FRIESIAN

A joke ought to have a
sheep's teeth, not a dog's

CZECH

If one person tells thee, thou hast
ass's ears, take no notice;
should two tell thee so,
procure a saddle for thyself

HEBREW

Seize opportunity by the beard
for it is bald behind

BULGARIAN

He who speaks the truth should
have one foot in the stirrup

HINDI (INDIA)

Do not go with a large basket
to over-praised strawberries

BULGARIAN

The seaman is right,
so is the landsman

ESTONIAN

Beware of a man
with a long chin

SPANISH

A friend spits into
a friend's pocket

ESTONIAN

He who goes to sea without
biscuits returns without teeth

CORSICAN

He who does not
eat cheese will go mad

FRENCH

One should not board a ship
without an onion

DUTCH

Do not burn down your house to
inconvenience even your
chief wife's mother

CHINESE

Do not remove a fly from your
friend's forehead with a hatchet

CHINESE

When the bed is small,
lie in the centre

SPANISH

A crab does not beget a bird

GA (WEST AFRICA)

Why should a man without
a head want a hat?

CHILEAN

The poor man and the fire
do not like to be poked

GALLA (NORTH AFRICA)

You may ride a horse well,
but don't try to sit
on your horse's head

BAMBARA (WEST AFRICA)

Never feed a dog with corn,
nor attempt to pick your teeth
with a pair of scissors

CHINESE

No one carrying elephant's flesh
on his head should look for
crickets underground

YORUBA (WEST AFRICA)

He who has only his
eyebrow for a crossbow
never can kill an animal

YORUBA (WEST AFRICA)

He who lives longest
has the most old clothes

ZULU (SOUTH AFRICA)

Do not stab yourself because
you have a golden knife

MARATHI (INDIA)

What is heaviest
should weigh heaviest

DUTCH

In a fight sweetmeats
are not distributed

HINDI (INDIA)

It is no use applying eye-medicine
from a two-storey window

JAPANESE

The man with nostrils is
Mr Nose amongst the noseless

HINDI (INDIA)

One must walk a long time behind
a wild duck before one picks
up an ostrich feather

DANISH

He who licks the saucepans at
home will not be killed in battle

CZECH

Mix thyself with bran
and thou shall be eaten by pigs

BOSNIAN

Kindness to the starfish is
as wind in the desert

CHINESE

God preserve us from pitchforks,
for they make three holes

SWISS

A stranger is like rain:
he strikes you then passes on

EAST AFRICAN

Govern a great nation as
you would cook a small fish

CHINESE

He who eats alone, coughs alone

EGYPTIAN

The law has a nose of wax

CZECH

What a pleasure to sit in the fire,
having on strange trousers

ESTONIAN

He who would make the
hole under his nose bigger
must wear patched shoes

DANISH

Baghdad is far away,
but the foot-rule is here

BOSNIAN

He who sows peas on the highway
doesn't get all the pods
into the barn

DANISH

Give a dog an appetising name
and eat him

CHINESE

He puts his cheese in a bottle
and rubs the cheese
on the outside

IRAQI

When the deaf gives the blind
a lamp he receives bagpipes

GERMAN

Don't let your sorrow come higher
than your knees

SWEDISH

When you take a squirrel
out of water, it contrives
a plot against you

DUALA (WEST AFRICA)

He who writes love letters
should have damp hands

GERMAN

He who eats old bread
will swim easily

RUSSIAN

During the cat's harvest,
hens are deaf

DUTCH

She is a foolish woman
who blames her own cabbage

DANISH

Fool your wife, use your bride,
teach your children to eat coal

ESTONIAN

Rest after a meal, even
if your parents are dead

JAPANESE

What goes wrong in the stable
falls on the monkey's head

INDIAN

Don't open your mouth
until a goose has flown in

ICELANDIC

Feigned laughter ruins the teeth

TAMIL (INDIA)

A farthing hag got her
head shaved for a penny

INDIAN

Better the gurgling of a camel
than the prayers of a fish

EGYPTIAN

When the mouse eats the stone pot,
the pumpkin skin gets alarmed

EWE (WEST AFRICA)

The Gypsy church was made of pork
and the dogs ate it

ROMANY

Many complaints have made
the giant lizard deaf

DUALA (WEST AFRICA)

A good buttock finds
a bench for itself

ESTONIAN

Do not blame God for having created the tiger, but thank Him for not having given it wings

ETHIOPIA

An early bird wipes its beak;
a late one wipes its buttocks.

ESTONIAN

If you do what people tell you,
you will be fishing hares
in the sea and hunting fish
in the woods.

BULGARIAN

He who eats cherries with his superiors will have pips thrown in his face

DANISH

A well-tinted lie counts
for the truth

SWEDISH

When you have figs in your haversack everybody seeks your friendship

ALBANIAN

When you go to a donkey house
don't talk about ears

JAMAICAN

Beware the foreparts of a woman,
the hindparts of a mule,
and all sides of a priest

ENGLISH

He who spits towards the sky
gets it back in his own face

THAI

A straight road has no turning

EFIK (WEST AFRICA)

When a donkey is well off
he goes dancing on ice

CZECH

Whilst the sheep bleats,
it loses a mouthful

FLEMISH

When the shepherds quarrel,
the cheese shows it

BASQUE

A woman for duty,
a boy for pleasure,
but a goat for ecstasy

TURKISH

If I be a queen
and thou be a queen,
who will bang the butter?

PUNJABI (INDIA)

Three things to cross the road
to avoid: a falling tree; your chief
and second wife whispering in
agreement; and a goat
wearing a leopard's tail

PRION HUMOUR

If you are interested in receiving details about Prion's humour titles ranging from postcard books to quotation books on all subjects to the Prion Humour Classics series, please write to the freepost address below, with the details of your name and address. You will receive a regular newsletter containing forthcoming title information, reviews, extracts and special offers. Please note that the freepost address only applies to correspondents within the United Kingdom, when no stamp is required. Overseas readers should please use our full address and the correct postage.

For UK correspondents:
Prion Humour
FREEPOST LON12574
London NW5 1YR

or email your details to: humour@prion.co.uk